MW00884669

Copyright © 2019 Heather Coleman

All rights reserved. No part of this publication may be reproduced or distributed in any form or by any means, or stored in a database or retrieval system, without the prior written permission of the author, except where permitted by law.

Legal & Disclaimer

The information contained in this book is not designed to replace or take the place of any form of medication or professional medical advice. The information in this book has been provided for educational and entertainment purposes only.

The information contained in this book has been compiled from sources deemed reliable, and it is accurate to the best of the Author's knowledge. However, the Author cannot guarantee its accuracy and validity so cannot be held liable for any errors or omissions. Changes are periodically made to this book. You must consult your doctor or get professional medical advice before using any of the suggested remedies, techniques, or information in this book.

Upon using the information contained in this book, you agree to hold harmless the Author from and against any damages, costs and expenses, including any legal fees, potentially resulting from the application of any of the information provided by this guide. This disclaimer applies to any damages or injury caused by the use and application, whether directly or indirectly, of any advice or information presented, whether for breach of contract, tort, negligence, personal injury, criminal intent, or under any other cause of action.

You agree to accept all the risks of using the information presented inside this book. You need to consult a professional medical practitioner in order to ensure you are both able & healthy enough to participate in this program.

Contents

Introduction

You heard a hard knock at your door and when you acknowledged it, a neighbor told you, 'You better see your child quick!' Your heart rate quickened in consonance with your steps as you headed to the neighbor's house where your child was attending a birthday party. Then you saw your 5-year-old cowered in a corner, trembling arms wrapped around folded knees with head bent between them. You immediately enveloped your child in a warm embrace and whispered, 'It's okay, sweetheart, I'm here,' as you gently run your hand on your child's head for comfort. Later you learned that everything seemed fine until the other children started the raucous party activities.

Such a child reaction usually shouldn't be a cause for alarm, but if you find your kid repeatedly exhibiting the adverse reaction when confronted with stimuli, you might have an empath child.

So, what is an empath child? Does it differ from being emphatic? Is being easily overwhelmed the only sign of being an empath?

Read on because this e-Book would be your indispensable companion in YOUR journey of self-discovery. Yes, in order to better understand your empath child, YOU need to walk the path of an empath.

Chapter 1 – How to Assess If Your Child Has the Empathic Gift

Know the Emphatic Gift

While most perceive that being an empath and emphatic are synonymous, the distinction is great. An emphatic person is someone who could relate to how another is feeling – and this shouldn't be mistaken with being sympathetic as well.

As a case in point, when you see a beggar barely sheltered under a bridge or their shaky hands stretched for a morsel of food, you feel sorry for the person's plight – this is sympathy. When you could feel the chill seep to your bones that a tattered overall barely wards off, that is empathy. But as an empath, the feeling is exponentially heightened – the chill comes with a fear of not having a home or going to sleep with an empty stomach.

Empaths are Highly Sensitive People (HSP) who also are clairsentients – they sense and assimilate the emotional energy of the people around them to the point of getting overwhelmed by the accompanying sensations, without using their five senses. This was best depicted in the book 'Diary of a Teenage Empath.' There was an exemplified scene when an HSP felt equally sad when a friend's dog died. An empath who neither knew nor heard the conversation could be overwhelmed with sadness by simply 'absorbing' the energy of the pair. So, what is the rationale behind such a reaction?

An empath's nervous system is like a mega computer that processes algorithms exponentially faster than ordinary desktops. Therefore, an empath's response to external stimuli is quicker than most people and is non-filtering. Meaning, an empath cannot choose what stimuli to react to – positive or negative. Moreover, empaths don't just react – they absorb the emotions of other people. The sponging causes an overload of the senses because empaths experience emotions more than non-empaths. However, there are training strategies that could be leveraged to maximize an empath's ability.

Acknowledge the Signs

If your child had undergone training as an empath, the succeeding signs may seem like a walk down memory lane – a sort of 'Ah, yes, I can relate' kind of vibe. Otherwise, the following list would aid you in properly addressing your concerns – whether you already know that you have an empath child or not.

- Experiences pain or extreme emotion - Your child complains of pains that have no physical manifestations or an intense emotion that seems baseless. However, you realize later that that was how you or another family member felt a few hours ago.

- Exhibits physical symptoms – In connection with the above sign, your child may exhibit stomach aches or headaches as a coping mechanism to express a feeling.

- Stimuli overload – A crowd overwhelms an empath child – the conversations, the mingling scents, and every emotion displayed by the people in the crowd – and your child sees these sensory stimulants as if they were being viewed from a Hobo telescope with great magnification.

- Loves to read and learn – Empath children continually thirst for knowledge and information.

- Lucid dreamers – Vivid dreams start early in life for empath children. Their dreams are so intense that they often perceive them as 'scary' nightmares. But even if their dreams aren't frightening, the effect is still very strong.

- Heightened sensitivity to other people's emotion – When in a crowd, familiar or not, your child absorbs every emotion of the people around. Your child may rush towards someone who was crying or attempt to comfort another person who was upset.

- Heightened personal emotions – Unlike non-empath kids, empath children feel deeply than others. While most children would simply shrug off a scolding, empath children could be devastated and possibly feel that they have disappointed their parents.

- Overly responsible – While a sense of responsibility in a child is amiable, empath children take it to greater heights that defy age appropriateness. They feel that they need to ensure other people's happiness and go out of their ways to help others. Empath children may also worry over things beyond their control like a mortgage payment or unsettled bills.

- Thinks excessively – Sometimes perceived as constant daydreaming, empath children tend to spend too much time thinking.

- Drawn to nature – The healing effect of nature is doubly calming for empaths, so they are drawn towards exploring the natural world. Empaths love to nurture life by growing things and observing animals inhabiting naturally.

- Lovers of art and music – While these may seem common even among non-empaths, empath children use these as channels to vent their excessive energies.

- More in-tune with animal friends – Empath children gravitate more with non-human friends like cats, dogs, or hamsters than with other children.

- Anthropomorphist – Empath children would stop you from throwing away a broken toy, thinking that it might feel hurt or unloved.

- Non-conformity to the norm – Empath children inadvertently feel 'out of place' even around kids their age that urge them not to mingle voluntarily.

- A semblance of a bipolar disorder – shifting moods in swift succession which only manifests when in a crowd or a big group of people.

- Evasion of certain people – Your child tries to stay away from some people who aren't exactly strangers, even familiar family members.

- Solitude is their best friend – Empaths need a lot of alone time.

- Lack of focus on activities when there are people around that usually were done smoothly when your child is left alone.

- Could blurt out observations about people that 'fit to a T' which otherwise wouldn't have been evident under normal conditions.

- Acting out as another person's character when around that person but reverts to old self when the person leaves.

- Couldn't identify an exact need or want unless you voice it out yourself.

- Struggles with own emotions because the emotions belonging to the people around greatly impacts and mingles with your child's own.

Recognize Challenges

About 15-20% of our population is HSP and only 2-4% are clairsentients. The numbers may seem insignificant but remember that these are in relevance to a conglomerate of billions. The bigger remaining percentage is the 'ruling' commonality that you and your empath child need to be incorporated with – and that poses a great challenge.

If you are a trained and/or an adult empath, you may even feel 'proud' with your extraordinary ability to read facial gestures, understand body languages, and seemingly walk another person's path. But while adults are generally more attuned to their own emotions, children aren't. In the eyes and mind of a child, these unique skills are frightening to possess because they are experiencing a lot of things simultaneously, magnified a thousand-fold. It's like they are tiny vessels being filled with maelstroms of emotions that they could barely understand. And in addition to the confusion, empath children are exposed to viewpoints of adults not familiar with empaths that perceive your child's intuitive abilities as an 'unnatural' deviation of the commonly accepted human interaction.

If your child isn't of schooling age yet, the scope of divergence may only be limited within family members and close neighbors. Otherwise, the circumference of struggling 'to fit' may expand to affect your child's academic and social connection.

Your empath child's abilities are there to stay. They are not like 'imaginary childhood friends' that your kid would outgrow or go away if ignored. It is prudent that you recognize your child's gift and learn to leverage to your child's advantage. Struggling to fight your child's innate talent may cause more damage than help because you would essentially be 'disintegrating' what makes your child a whole human being.

The challenge would be great from the onset because it may seem that despite your relentless heart-to-heart talk with your child about the gift, the overwhelming sensation manages to keep coming back. Note that shifting perspectives is hard even for adults, so don't expect immediate results with your child. You may have leveraged special techniques – on your own or through a medical practitioner – to alleviate your child's emotional struggle, but there would be occasions when you would feel that the situation reverts to where you started or that you hit the wall of stagnation. When you do, recognize that you are dealing with both the psychological and energetic levels of your child. Empath training is the tool to specifically target these aspects of your child's empath ability manifestations.

At this point, it would be prudent to stress avoiding the pitfall of 'passing-the-buck.' True, your empath child sponges the emotions of people around. But should these people be blamed? If you do, you might as well set-up camp atop a mountain where the only human interaction that your child would experience would be with you. Human interaction would always be integral in the normalcy of your child's life. And empath training would aid in your child's transition to mingling without being overwhelmed. There wouldn't be specific guidelines in distinguishing another's emotion from your child's own. However, as you progress with your child's training, there would be practicing strategies that would ease you both out; you just must leverage these techniques one at a time.

Chapter Quiz

1. Are empaths and emphatic people the same?

2. Could an empath choose what stimuli to react to?

3. Could empaths absorb the emotions and energies of the people around them?

4. Is physical pain manifestation without symptoms common in an empath?

5. Do empaths personify inanimate objects or animals as if they are humans with feelings?

Chapter 2 – Easing Out Your Emphatic Child's Emotions and Energy

Address Your Child's Abilities

There is one basic fact that you need to orient yourself with for you to effectively help your empath child ease out of an eternal fountain of emotions – Energy.

Energy is real and you could perceive it with your physical senses. It takes several forms and it includes emotions and physical sensations that could move between and among people. For an empath, the transfer of energy is quick and exponential. Your child is like a sponge that absorbs and assimilates these energies without filter – whether they were conducive or otherwise. To top that, they mingle with your child's own. Here is where you come in. While you couldn't consciously sieve which energy 'gets in,' you could help your child understand that it's a gift that the two of you could explore together.

However, it wouldn't be an easy journey to travel. So much had been researched and discussed on being an empath – the tribulations and the joys. But regrettably, most perceived being an empath as an affliction that required protection from others' negativity. It defies what an empath is – a 'magnet' of other's woes because it's integrated deeply into an empath's subconscious mind to 'feel.' And it's a powerful ability that should be nurtured, not embedded with fear.

Easier said than done, right? I couldn't agree more because the automatic response to deflect negativity is deeply seated in our DNAs – the cortisol doing its job in our fight-or-flight defense mechanism. But with your empath child's heightened nervous system, the influx of outside energy is equally potent. When you attempt to shield your kid from these 'invasive' forces, you are consequently gearing your child to fight what is innate and the effect could be disorienting. It would be like making your child's right and left brain hemispheres to clash with one another – the part that yearns to feel and the part that refuses to. Instead of easing out your empath child's emotions, you would be draining your kid's energy to effectively assimilate the inevitable.

So, what would be a more conducive approach in addressing your empath child's abilities? Critically observe what dominates your child's empath expression. What types of stimuli trigger your child's response more quickly? Is it a spontaneous loud commotion? How about a big crowd? Or perhaps a situation that purports melancholy? Think of this along the lines of 'everything in moderation.' If your empath child already has a substantial reservoir of a certain emotion, an influx of the same emotion trigger could break the dam. And since building a fortress around your child isn't the best resort, start from within. Help your child understand about emotions innate to empaths. It would be like caring for a deep wound – slowly nurture until the pain subsides. When you allow your empath child to heal (understand the empath abilities), your kid would have a better grasp of the empath gift, consequently developing the ability to assimilate outside-influenced emotions without the jolt. Always remember the keyword MODERATION. Take it slow. You couldn't expect a deep wound to heal overnight, right? The same principle applies to address your empath child's abilities. It would only be after your child had understood how heightened an empath's emotions are that the diverse stimuli offered by the outside world would cease to overwhelm. Your child would turn to perceive outside emotions as mere reflections of those innate within your kid. Expect that it would be a challenge both for you and, to a greater extent, your child. But it would be the right path to start with.

Contrary to what the world wide web suggests of shielding your child against the negative stimuli, make it your starting point. Instead of veering away, analyze how your child reacts when around people that impact your child negatively but be readily available to guide. Once your child's resistance of the outside stimuli is broken, the energy transfer could be a smooth transition. Furthermore, it may even be plausible for your child to develop a 'personal sieve' – from regulating the flow of energy to selectively allowing what energy to assimilate.

Remember, you would be attempting to 'break' an existing pattern that your child had been living. And expectedly, you would encounter resistance. Don't barge the wall with a wrecking ball a la Miley Cyrus. Have patience and acknowledge the essentiality of a smooth transition.

Be WITH Your Child

As an empath, your child may be obsessed with someone. Recognize that this isn't some sporadic compulsion inside your child's head. Chances are, there is a plethora of subconscious energy flow between your child and the object of fixation. Also know that as an empath who gets deeply affected by someone, your child does not simply imagine how it's like to be the other person, your child may literally be absorbing the other person's energy. And simply telling your child that a change must be done would be like dropping a bomb on your homeland.

Therefore, your active participation in the fundamental shift in your child's life is crucial. Despite the yottabyte of information on the internet, being an empath is a struggle that no amount of scientific research could lessen the blow of a radical change – that responsibility falls on YOU as a parent. While studies could equip you with a selection of 'tools' to help your empath child adapt to the 'influential' world, remember the existential diversity of people, more so when one is an empath. Strategies claimed to be effective may not hold true with your child. Ergo, examine your choices well and always take into consideration what matters most – YOUR CHILD.

Understand and Guide Your Child

Even trained and experienced empaths are uncertain which of their emotions are their own and which are from the people they connect with. While it's innate for an empath to assimilate the emotions of people around, understanding that your child has this capacity would guide you towards raising your child's awareness of said innate gift. We tend to fear the unknown and an empath's ability ranks high on that scale. Why? Because it had been hammered in on us since we were young that the emotions we feel are entirely OUR own. Therefore, people who are unaware of an empath's gift veer towards uncertainty and general paranoia when confronted by its manifestation. When you see your child withdraw in a corner during a family gathering, what is your initial interpretation? Fear of a crowd or of unfamiliar faces? If your child is an empath, it goes beyond that. Your child could be assimilating all the emotions of the people around and is experiencing an overload of inexplicable energy that mingles with your child's own. Even if you have been intervening in your child's empath gift early on, your child's awareness of the conflicting emotions runs deep and could still be too confusing to analyze for a child.

Remember how energy flows from one person to another? To an empath, energies don't just flow – they stick. Meaning, your empath child juggles within not only emotions from people connections now, but from other people that your child had connected with in the past. And due to the very nature of these outside emotions latching on to your child's own, the possibility is great that your child may interpret the emotions as indeed self-expressions. You also need to understand that other people's emotions don't differ from your child's or yours. Emotions are 'generic' in the sense that we all feel sad, angry, excited, and scared. The similarity adds to the confusion in differentiating which emotions belong to other people and which are your child's own. There is no dating-site-like feature of 'swipe left or right' of categorizing the source of the energy. As a result, your empath child's deep sensitivity would readily 'accept' incoming emotions as part of your child's being. The cruciality of understanding your child's empath ability, therefore, catapults it as the most integral part of giving your child a life not fearing the outside world.

Chapter Quiz

1. Could empaths distinguish between their own emotions and those of the people around them?

2. Are training tools available for empaths applicable to all?

3. Is it possible for an empath to obsess with someone or fixate on something?

4. Would shielding your empath child from the world's negativity your best option?

5. Could you transfer your own emotions to your empath child unconsciously?

Chapter 3 – Be Your Emphatic Child's Mentor

Boost Your Child's Self-Worth

With all those 'absorbed' emotions and energy, unfamiliarity with an empath gift, and being overwhelmed by it all, your child quite reasonably would develop a deteriorated self-confidence. But what would you expect? To have a high regard of one's self, one should confidently feel good deep inside. With the amalgamation of emotions and energy from other people mingling with your child's own, the confusion could easily rattle your child's young mind and develop into a low self-regard. There might even be manifestations in the form of physical pains.

How could you expect your child to 'feel good' with all those emotions playing tag? Often, it's easy for your kid's confidence to spiral down because of non-familiarity of what was going on and how to handle the confusion.

Orient Your Child of the Outside World

Unless you intend a life of seclusion for your child, interacting with the outside world is inevitable. As your child mingles with people who are not oriented with an empath ability, don't be surprised with reactions of curiosity, condescension, and evasion. While you feeling hurt for your child is understandable, nurturing the emotion would just provide another negative energy for your child to 'suck on.' And as an empath, your child could easily sense your worry, which means you couldn't hide your own emotions. Empaths could pick-up even the most subtle of cues like a side glance to hide a facial expression or slight discomfort, causing them to feel stressed. On the other hand, if you would opt to perceive that other people simply are not aware of your child's gift, you, in turn, are teaching your child to practice the same mindset.

Working with your child's empath ability would require dedicating time and effort. It might seem like a tough feat but choose to see it as a challenge worth working on. Commitment is crucial as always. Your child's integration into the society may seem dim at first, but with training, easing your child to connect with the world outside is an influential factor in reversing the sense of being overwhelmed. Ironic as it may sound, you need to expose your child to the very source of the emotion influx to be equipped with a refocused response in handling the energy inflow.

The world might label your empath child as shy, sensitive, or even thought to be depressed. While it might be the case, it's up to you as a parent to bring out the best in your child. How? Acknowledge that your child's sensitivity is an expression of compassion with so much depth – an ability to be so in-tune with other people that their emotions and feelings rub off on your child.

Leverage Your Child's Emphatic Abilities for Success

You are either certain or have a feeling that your child has the empath gift. So, what now? As a parent, it falls upon you to acknowledge and aid your child to live a happy life by leveraging the unique gift. Given the small percentage of empaths in the world as mentioned under 'Recognize the Challenges,' it's enough to say that so is the empath gift. Sadly, the remaining greater percentage of the world perceives empaths as too emotional, highly sensitive, or extremely needy. And since your child sponges these perceptions, growing up without the proper training could psychologically impact your child's adult life later. Therefore, it depends on YOU to ensure that love and support are constants as your child grows up and guide your child to embrace the gift instead of resenting it. And contrary to common notions, your empath child's success in life shouldn't start in adulthood. Your support in dealing with your child's overwhelming emotions shouldn't vary depending on just the age but on the level of your child's growth in adapting to the gift.

- Keep the communication line open with your child – no sense in 'hiding' from them anyway. The more you attempt to hide when something is amiss, the more that your child will perceive the worse, thinking that you are withholding something. Your child may even take the blame as a result of being an empath. Whenever an issue arises, openly talk it out with your child while taking your child's age into regard. Just be reassuring that you would handle the situation as ably as you could so your child need not worry.

- When your child appears to be overly sensitive and dramatic, don't take them lightly. It might be an indirect way of asking for help from you. And the overstated display of emotions might be your child's way of trying to cope with the plethora of feelings and emotions that your child is experiencing. Show your support and sympathy by using kind words, a hug, or a kiss to comfort and reassure your child.

- If headaches or stomach aches are frequent with your child yet medical findings show no source, don't invalidate the ailments. Have you ever felt so nervous that you must visit the bathroom countless times, but nothing came out? Multiply that feeling several times over and you'd understand how your empath child feels. When empath children experience sensory overload, it manifests into physical ills if they couldn't express them out loud. Don't equate the physical ailments as attention-seeking. Scientific studies prove that stress could manifest as pains, and reassurance from parents could make empath children feel better.

- Encourage your child to relax and have fun when you sense your child's tendency to take on responsibilities. Remind your child that while caring for others is admirable, other people could handle their situations on their own.

- While it may seem awkward when your child hides behind your back when around people who aren't necessarily unfamiliar faces, don't construe this as a sign of shyness. An empath child could simply be assimilating your inner and unconscious reaction to the other person. It would be stressful for your child to be shoved forward to deflect your embarrassment. If your child is an empath, trust the child's instinct and reflect on your relationship with the person concerned. Who knows, maybe your empath child would be able to unearth your own hidden worries and reservations about the person.

- Most empaths couldn't imbibe a feeling of belongingness. In a society that dictates the norms, empath children perceive that they are 'different.' What may be common interests among kids their age may not hold true with them and it gives them a feeling of alienation. A redundant 'You're special' isn't the trick. It would make them feel even more ostracized, thinking that only you see them as extraordinary. Don't force them to conform just to be 'normal.' When you do, you'd be disintegrating their innate personality that could aggravate their feeling 'uncommon.'

- Solitude is empath children's best buddy. While non-empaths get bored when alone, empaths look forward to being alone to 'recover' from an overload of emotions and energy. Solitude sort of recharges your child's battery and a chance to heal from being burnt-out caused by the sensory surcharge. Even non-empaths and adults need to refill their energy bars after toiling a day's work. NEVER require your child to 'socialize' when you sense that your child is already experiencing an influx of emotions.

- Empath children often dream vividly. One way to get a handle of this is by keeping a dream journal. Jot down specifics of your child's dreams and use it as a reference to look back on and talk about when your child is more relaxed. Note recurring dreams or images that highlight the dreams. These could be manifestations of emotions that your child finds hard to process.

- Fear is a strong emotion and shouldn't be taken lightly, especially when it concerns an empath child. Your child may not always openly tell you of fear to save you from being worried, so be observant of your child's behavior. Immediately talk WITH – not to – your child as soon as you sense the manifestation of fright.

- Children aren't well articulated to express their thoughts. Therefore, as a parent, it's up to you to let your child understand and cope with the feelings. Be vigilant to learn the stimuli that easily set your child off. These could be people, activities, viewing programs, jam-packed days, or no alone time. As soon as you qualify the triggers, assist to lessen them as much as you could.

- When you find your empath child spending too much time thinking, like when your child sits still and stare at a singular space for an extended length of time, your child may be trying to analyze the outside world and how it deeply connects to your child's being. Don't try to disrupt the train of thoughts. Instead, ask your child about the thoughts and if your child willingly opens-up, listen attentively. Ask questions if you see fit to encourage your child to share thoughts. When empath children's deep thinking is actively engaged, instead of letting them process on their own, it harnesses their analytical nature even further, consequently gearing them towards a successful career as an adult.

- Support your empath child's profound interest to learn. Often, you'd find that empath children couldn't let go of a certain topic until they have learned more about it. They might start to read at a very young age and consider libraries as favorite hangouts. The key is encouraging support from parents. If you find that your interests don't match, say so honestly and perhaps meet halfway on topics that encompass both your interests.

- The arts and music are like volcano tips for empath children's 'lava buildup.' Especially among younger empaths who aren't articulate enough just yet, when they create or enjoy the arts and music, it is their way of self-expression. Support their energy outlet by providing them art materials or age-appropriate musical instruments to dabble on. Avoid saying, 'Oh, no!' when they spill a watercolor tube or smudge their overalls. When they present you with a Pollock-like painting, don't interpret it for them – ask them what it represents. Just don't buy them a grand piano if they ask for one. That would be going overboard – unless, of course, you need a bigger wallet for all your money.

- Introduce the practice of mindfulness meditation. Meditation is considered as a therapeutic exercise in grounding and centering one's self. This would be very beneficial if your child starts to spiral down after being overwhelmed. Dedicate a certain time in your child's day-to-day schedule for a 'decompression time.' You may choose a certain part of your home as your child's 'Zen space.'

- Another meditative technique that you could leverage is 5-Sense Meditation. This is most helpful when your child mirrors another person's pain. If your child couldn't identify a feeling of pain or hurt emotions, focus on what your child could smell, hear, see, touch, and taste. This technique would gradually bring your child back to the present. Once calmed, acknowledge your child's kindness for others then enjoin in some comforting activity for the both of you.

- Sometimes you'd notice that empath children would rather play with household pets than mingle with children in the neighborhood. This could be because unlike humans, animals have lesser body languages or emotions to sponge on. Pets are also known to reciprocate a human affection unconditionally. Don't hinder the attachment. Just ensure there wouldn't be allergy issues, with your empath child or any family member. It would be excruciatingly painful for your child if you must take away a

pet that your child had grown attached to simply because of allergic
reactions.

- Have you ever experienced having a tug o' war with your child over a
broken doll or toy truck? And even when you explain that you'd simply
buy a new one, your child worries that the old toy might cry. Recognize
that empath children think that even inanimate objects have feelings, too.
If your child is but a toddler (not older than four years old), there is no
harm in stitching back a frayed toy arm. But as your child gets older,
explain the concept of discarding something worn out as 'moving on.'
Say that older things may be given a new purpose even if they take on
new forms.

- Empath children's emotional response may be likened to multi-tiered
cakes – but their cake icings are more layered than most and too much of
it could crumble your child. If you must call your child's attention to a
misdemeanor, do so gently. Don't embarrass your child by scolding in
front of friends. If your child bounces off the wall in delight, don't
invalidate the elation. Instead, attempt to slow down the energy burst in a
manner that wouldn't seem like you're making fun of your child's
emotional response to being excited.

- Nurture your empath's child natural gravitation to anything nature. Let
your child's hands get dirty gardening or get soaked while playing with
water. Make outdoor activities integral in you and your child's bonding
time – go hiking or camping on tents under star-spangled skies.

- Let your child know that THERE IS NOTHING WRONG WITH
BEING AN EMPATH. Being more sensitive and intuitive than other
people are admirable abilities that only need to be honed for young people
like your child. Inform your child that while feelings about certain people
or situations may seem hard to control, it could be learned.

Being an Empath Is A Gift

Being an empath child isn't something that your child does, it's who your child is.
Most people may yet to perceive it so, but if empath children could be nurtured to
let their inner light shine, they could radiate their soulful gift to propagate

compassion on Earth. With proper guidance, empaths could cleanse the worldwide angst that haunts mankind. You may find it challenging to convince your empath children to work on themselves because they innately are givers. But if empaths, especially the young ones, could be taught to harness their gift to the fullest, they could transform other people's lives in an exponential manner.

- When empath children learn to better control their energy, their instinctive capabilities could even soar higher without feeling overwhelmed. Their innate sensitivity could be leveraged to acquire more wisdom.

- Empaths are outstanding in manifesting their energies. Their intentions and emotions are perfectly aligned.

- They are natural healers. It may not be evidently so early on, but with the right steering, their healing ability improves as they learn to channel their energies more effectively. They could leverage the energy flow to radiate a positive force through their hands or their voice.

- Empaths are greatly enthusiastic about life which allows them to experience happiness with far greater intensity. They are also more kind, compassionate, caring, and understanding.

- Because of the empaths' heightened sensory perception, they get to appreciate food and scents more intensely. At a more highly skilled level, empaths could even 'smell' health endangerment in people or animals, ultimately saving lives. On the same note, they could also sense potential dangers and be proactively ready.

- Empaths are great 'lie-detectors.' They could see through anyone and even through 'white lies' that most adults utilize when speaking to children.

- Unlike non-empaths, delving within is an easy task for trained empaths. They could readily tap their inner selves as they explore their gift.

- Empaths' unusual creativity allows them to conceptualize more easily as compared to non-empaths. This skill transcends the field of art and spills over to life events like experiences, situations, and possibilities.

- People with empath abilities could read emotional cues because they are very emotional themselves. Therefore, they could imagine what another person feels, and the possible outcome should the need be not met. They are highly sensitive to sense even non-verbal communications and this talent allows them to intuit into another's unconscious mind even if they don't have verbal capacities like animals.

- Empaths could thrive in a negative life polarity because with proper training, they could find strength in their power within to convert into a positive one.

- Other empaths have telepathic abilities. They could have premonitions of what is yet to happen and could instinctively gain information through their dreams.

- Empaths' ability to sponge other people's energies is rewarding in the sense that they could experience joy at heightened levels and enjoy emotional intimacy exceptionally. They could be totally in-tune with nature and possess an admirable trait of caring deeply for other people.

- People with the empath gift open-heartedly aim to make a difference in the lives of others. They unselfishly give assistance at homeless shelters or participate in drives to rescue ill-fated animals. Despite sometimes being misunderstood, empaths voluntarily lend a hand to people who need emotional support or those victimized by disasters or social injustice.

Successes Worth Emulating

The challenges of raising an empath child are both daunting and fulfilling. While your reactions sit on opposite sides of a beam, the focal point that sets the balance is your desire to give the best life for your empath child. And your child is already equipped with the essentials to succeed in life.

Built-in Success Triggers

- Ability to delve into another's thoughts – Whatever career that your child sees fit to embark on in the future, your child's ability to decipher another's thoughts is a plus. Empaths could sense what a colleague, business associate, or customer feels or needs. Therefore, your child could incorporate 'business with pleasure' by breaking down personality barriers.

- Maxed intuitive skills – On most occasions, empaths don't need to be told about certain things because they just know. They could sense the important things that need prioritizing. Their gut intuition is more to the point that translates to the immediate resolution of issues arising in the workplace or their own business ventures.

- Attentiveness – Empaths don't just hear but LISTEN. They don't let things just pass by them – they consciously process the information set before them.

- Focus – Trained empaths' innateness in shying away from being bombarded with an influx of emotions translates to having the ability to focus on a certain task at hand.

- Boredom detector – Empaths are drawn towards stimulants that are creative and passionate. When they sense boredom seeping in, they find ways to innovate and bring the spirit back into the game.

Successful Empaths

Empaths' gift of sensing other people's emotions and the intuition to know what another person may be feeling or thinking are but some of the determinants that propel people to succeed in life. It's a challenge to exactly pinpoint an empath, but here are some who openly admit that they are and some who are believed to be.

Katrina Pfannkuch *(https://creativekatrina.com/about/)*

If you would ask Katrina to describe herself, this is what she would say – creativity consultant and catalyst, intuitive guide, EMPATH, writer, content strategist, and podcaster. On her blog 'Grieve and Make Peace Before Creating a Fresh Path, she shared that 'When we grieve and make peace with what never came to pass, we can restart from a place of pure heart.' She further added that it was an enlightening and empowering experience to do so. In addition, she believed that starting anew was like an invitation to trekking a fresh path forward without past judgments and expectations.

Wan Ting, Quek (https://medium.com/swlh/living-as-an-empath-when-you-feel-everything-and-nobody-seems-to-understand-65fecce2aa03)

If you would read through Wan Ting's profile in Medium – The Startup, she admits being a dancing warrior who advocates for mental health through the power of movement. She also shares life lessons from her own journey. In her article 'Living as an Empath – when you feel everything and nobody seems to understand,' she said that she never liked using the term 'empath' in her practice as a counselor, despite being an empath herself. But the experience taught her that early recognition of empath abilities aided in the effective practice of her work. While she only got acquainted with the term 'empath' around 2010, it was when she grew older that she was able to identify herself with the word. It was then that she decided to work with people with the same abilities. She believes that the traits of an empath are among the gifts available to people – they just happen to be more intense on others. She further said that empath or not, people are gifts who have something unique that each possesses individually.

Jesus Christ

Not to speak out of bounds regarding diverse religious beliefs, Jesus Christ was the founder of Christianity and as of 2010, 2.2 billion Christians would agree that He epitomizes everything good about an empath. His life had been depicted to care for the poor and the sick. He had also been shown to be equally pained when others were. Yes, you couldn't expect your child to be God-like, but the exemplification is just to stress that the empath traits are worth emulating and assimilating.

Mahatma Gandhi

Gandhi felt strongly for the Indian people that he became a civil rights activist. His life was devoted to creating a positive change by leveraging non-violent civil non-conformity. He had the ability to connect with the Indian people by internalizing their struggles and sharing the pain they experienced. He so believed in effectively campaigning for Indian independence from the British rule that he threw away his fancy suit, wrapped himself a in loincloth, and lead an Ashram (peasant farmers) life from 1971 to 1930.

George Orwell

A colonial police officer in Burma in the 1920s, Orwell earned the 'empath star' when he witnessed firsthand the colonialism's brutality that urged him to assimilate the lives of working people to learn how their lives felt like. He was quoted to say, 'I wanted to submerge myself, to get right down among the oppressed; to be one of them and on their side against the tyrants.'

Claiborne Paul Ellis

Born into a poor family in Durham, North Carolina in 1927, CP Ellis's hammered-in belief that the blacks caused his life misfortune turned 180 degrees when in 1971, he met the black activist Ann Atwater in a 10-day community meeting to resolve school racial tensions. As head of the race committee, Ellis worked jointly with Atwater and learned that she, too, shared his impoverished roots. Their views also resonated with each other on how white businessmen and politicians kept wages low and pitted poor blacks and whites against one another. Ellis also said, 'I was beginning to look at a black person, shake hands with him, and see him as a human being.'

Harriet Beecher Stowe

This American novelist's empath trigger was slavery. Her book 'Uncle Tom's Cabin' that sold four million copies within a decade from 1852 was a product of her agony when her eighteen-month-old son Charley died of Cincinnati cholera epidemic in 1849. She greatly related to black women whose children were sold to slavery. Beecher Stowe said, 'It was at his bed, and at his grave, that I learnt what a poor slave mother may feel when her child is torn away from her.'

Chapter Quiz

1. Is it innate for empaths to care and give?

2. With proper training and guidance, could empaths heal others through their hands or encouraging words?

3. Could empath children read non-verbal cues?

4. Are saying 'white lies' effective to save your empath child from worrying?

5. Could your empath child succeed in life?

6. As you learn to understand your empath child, could you also learn from your child's empath gift?

7. Could an empath survive a negative environment without the support of the parents or a strategic training?

8. Is it easy for untrained empaths to understand their 'fountain' of emotions?

9. Do empath children gravitate more towards non-human interactions?

10. Is meditation an effective way to lessen the impact of sensory overload?

Conclusion

People are divergent from one another, empath or no empath. And within the close circle of highly sensitive people, the dissimilarity could even be more pronounced. While this eBook aims to be as specific as possible, the signs and suggested steps may find resonance in some parents and not applicable to some.

However, the intent is clear – be as honest as possible with your empath child. Your child will always 'see through you' no matter how hard you try to hide. Of course, it's not an implication that you're free to unload all your woes to your kid. Instead, learn to acknowledge your own troubles and give your child the assurance that you would handle the situation the best way that you could.

Your empath child deals with emotions that are sometimes overwhelming even for adults. Even with a young age, your child's innate heightened sensitivity pushes your child to cope. So, don't just hear when your kid speaks – LISTEN. Shower your child with love and affection the way any parent should.

And remember, be true to yourself first because a sugar-coated truth would not elicit a positive response from your empath child. But you would know if you are on the right track if your child starts to smile, relax, and enjoy playing as most children do. After all, a happy childhood is a sturdy foundation for conducive adult life.

Children with the empath gift view the world with a unique set of eyes. And just like 'regular' kids, they deserve to be acknowledged, cared for, and understood.

Your empath child perceives emotions at a level quite different from others. Embrace it because that is who your child is – a rare gem who could potentially change the world to be a more compassionate home. Be proud to be raising one because the world, in my opinion, needs more empaths than it cares to admit. ALWAYS BE THERE FOR THEM.

Seven-Step Action Plan

In support of everything that we discussed in this eBook, below is a bird's eye view on helping your empath children succeed early on in life that would serve as a sturdy foundation for their adulthood.

- The first step is to acknowledge that empaths exist. When you recognize the manifestations in your child, accept that you have an empath child and actively listen.

25

- Acknowledge that empaths have a wide range of emotions – their own and those of others – without passing judgment. Nevertheless, don't be afraid to be vulnerable around your child because it accords your child the feeling of normalcy.

- Don't suppress your child's expression of emotions. But when your child experiences sensory overload, know that it would take time before the overwhelming sensations dissipate.

- Spend quality time with your empath child and teach your child to understand the empathic gift before encouraging to understand the emotions of people around.

- Leverage specialized training techniques for empaths, even if you think you could handle it on your own.

- Acknowledge that being an empath is a gift because only then could you truly encourage your empath child to believe so. And be an empath yourself, a model whom your child could emulate.

- ALWAYS prioritize to protect your child by showing unconditional love and affection.

We all were innately empathic when we were children. However, the 'toxicity' of the world we live unconsciously hammered the innateness is us that drove it too far down in the deep recesses of our mind. This is our chance to bring back the children in us as we nurture our empath children, so they won't lose their empathic nature.

-- Heather Coleman

Made in the USA
Columbia, SC
04 April 2021

35628906R00015